EPIPHANY MARKETING

EPIPHANY MARKETING

THE HEART OF MARKETING STARTS AT YOUR CORE

BY DR. MAISHA COBB

First Edition, 2019
Printed in the United States of America
ISBN: 9781097615407

DEDICATION

This book is dedicated to all of you who dare to dream outside the box in effort, and with intent, to move humanity forward (in small and big ways), to those allow others the freedom to think beyond barriers, and to those who inspire greatness in the soul. I don't know most of you, but I trust that your efforts are helping us all move closer to a world of better humanity.

The world needs you so, thank you!

CONTENTS

ACKNOWLEDGMENTS

I would like to express my deep gratitude to all those who continue to help me visualize a life not yet realized as well as those who keep me connected to the lessons already learned.

Carson, thank you for reminding me daily to be authentic and honest. Mom and Dad for the solid foundation and encouragement to always push beyond perceived obstacles. Trina, Zeretha and Michael, thank you for your quiet, unyielding support. And finally, Doug – though you are no longer here – thank you for the magnificent gift of remembrance that we all have a duty to serve and though it may look different, that service matters.

PREFACE

In 1995, I had the great fortune of working for a non-profit organization that lived and breathed its purpose of bringing awareness (and change) to the incidence of HIV/AIDS that was rapidly spreading among heterosexual women of color in Los Angeles. Many of the women we served were forgotten and unaddressed by many of the existing programs. The organization was started by two very spunky social justice leaders, but in a very short time they had amassed an impressive fan base consisting of employees, community leaders, clients and donors, all who believed in the mission and personally committed to the purpose.

As I write this, the thoughts and experiences of my time at Prototypes still give me warm feelings of excitement and hope. The exhilaration of knowing what we were able to collectively accomplish, the positive impact that our work brought to so many lives. We were not paid much, sometimes grants did not work out, but we were empowered by a mission so much bigger than us all.

This mission fueled a passion that led us to become true advocates who effortlessly committed every day to improve lives at that moment, and in the future. This isn't a fairytale, as some of my close friends died of AIDS and others could not mentally escape the boundaries of their mind that kept them stuck. Despite these realities, the commitment to changing another's journey for the better was contagious. The work we did led to recognition beyond what any of us could have imagined – on a local, statewide and national stage.

I often connect with my friends LaFonda, Paula and Tina, with whom I shared that experience, and we are still invigorated by the memories of making our mark. I've eagerly approached each new opportunity expecting the same fervor, the same committed passion and the same belief that we were doing something that really can change lives.

I live in gratitude for each and every moment of my career journey, but I am most grateful for the opportunity to work for and consult with amazing organizations that are truly doing brilliant things to improve the world.

Reflecting on the numerous organizations I've encountered and specifically on those that passed my Prototypes passion and authenticity test, my aim to share a new marketing approach that builds on these models and starts with you.

Marketing has as much to do with the souls of these organizations, as the missions they often profess. You see, there is energy that is living and breathing in organizations and if that energy gets too disconnected from original purpose, core beliefs - no amount of marketing will resonate. That energy needs to be reclaimed and reconnected.

I wrote this book at a time in my own life when I was searching to rediscover myself, my life's passion and redefine my own core. I had lost my connection to social and environmental causes, and I was desperate to evolve creatively, spiritually and personally. As a leader, I was struggling to find my voice and found myself saying the *right and acceptable* words but lacking the passion behind the semantics. I found myself longing to reconnect with others who also wanted to connect with something bigger, something more meaningful and something a whole lot more real.

I believe in the power of relevant Marketing, but during this time I found myself becoming more disillusioned with the practice. I began to feel an internal rebellion rising each time I experienced the vast amount of content that was coming at me every day, not wanted and not relatable.

This book is short but with purpose. It is less about teaching how to do marketing – there are plenty of resources out there for that – and much more about helping the leaders of organizations, marketers and individuals to rediscover a deeper purpose, to find their own voice and to share that unique voice with the broader world. The message is simple – marketing your core is the only viable option to success, but requires you to have a deep awareness, as well as honesty and courage.

I share this with the hope that it will inspire you to have the audacity to reconnect with your passion and use that deep fervor to fuel your marketing, your organizations and yourselves.

CHAPTER 1

Epiphany – (Merriam Dictionary definition) – a usually sudden manifestation or perception of the essential nature or meaning of something, or an intuitive grasp of reality through something (such as an event) usually simple and striking, or an illuminating discovery, realization, or disclosure.

EPIPHANIES AND MARKETING

As I recall various events that occurred over the course of my own life, epiphanies were usually very important, yet very undervalued, parts of my experience. You see, epiphanies are these rare synchronistic, "what the heck just happened," moments that often led me down a specific path or opened my eyes to something that I had yet to realize.

Epiphanies have the power to change your perspective drastically and awaken discovery to a whole new point of view that you had been ignoring until that moment. The insight that these moments provided often led me to pay attention or make a conscious choice to do something different or take a bold leap of faith.

As leaders of organizations, and particularly in marketing, we often neglect to pay attention to these jarring gut moments, and instead rely heavily on our rational minds to guide what we do. However, through my 20 years of marketing, I've concluded that this is a mistake. You see the very essence of marketing and leadership is to realize that there is no secret sauce, no recipe book for leading or marketing – it is a feeling or emotion that becomes infectious, that galvanizes others, and creates your momentum.

Momentum usually starts within the walls of your organization, but the depth of momentum created is reflective of your commitment to sharing your true core. The aim of this book is to get you back in touch with the less rational side of your organization so you can make the most out of it, and find your way to the true power of your core (gut/intuition) when it comes to leadership in marketing (and overall).

What is marketing?

When I ask various leaders to describe "marketing" through the lens of their organizations, as you can imagine, there are multiple levels of detail in their responses. Sometimes it is described as an art and sometimes it is a science. Often, it is described as a prescribed way of communicating or showcasing a specific set of capabilities and/or services. It is inextricably linked with how organizations project and protect their brand (the tangible and intangible elements that makes them special) image.

Today, the field of marketing is almost always associated with various digital technologies. This is unfortunate because technology is a very rational, practical and scientific application that relies on methods and processes versus having the fluidity to connect on a much more personal level. As a result, technology has introduced a rigidity that undermines fluidity.

Marketing is the action of promoting products or services and relies heavily on telling a story.

Sounds rational right? Well it is and it isn't, and therein lays the problem. We have over rationalized marketing to the point that emotion has left the practice and what remains are impersonal attempts to throw lots of content at fans – the individuals who are most meaningful for your organization like board members, clients, employees, customers, funders, donors, external collaborators, etc. – in effort to see what sticks. What gets lost, however, is the emotion of marketing - the need to connect values with behavior and choice.

If rationality has overtaken your marketing, you are not alone. By reading this book, you've taken the first step in a journey to realize that marketing is much more than creating content to see what sticks. The first step begins with understanding that marketing is energetic and emotional. Without either of those ingredients, rationality will overtake and impede your ability to make a real connection.

Marketing today is about a few things:

- Creating experiences and driving change. Discover why and how you make a change in people's lives, in your community, in the world – and communicate it.

- Understanding and articulating the impact your organization has on your immediate surroundings and beyond, as well as how you can use this platform to improve broader societal outcomes.

- Connecting with your fans in a manner that means something for them. It is important to always think about fans when making decisions regarding a call to action or a course of action towards them.

The challenge is that as leaders, we often get stuck in myopic thinking about our organization (mission, purpose, actions) and ultimately behave the same way year in and year out. The same or worse can happen when it comes to those we support or who support us. In this evolving world, it's critical that you remember that your fans, like your organizations, change too.

I wrote this book because I believe everyone can do great marketing. It starts with a compelling story to tell, and it creates value for those who it reaches. Let's roll up our sleeves and have some real talk about marketing, where we are, where we are going, and reasons why.

The benefit of trusting your gut

Imagine a time when you went with your gut. Think about the feelings, the sensations and the related thoughts that accompanied those moments when something "just felt right or wrong." Often, we can't explain why something feels right or wrong, but it turns out that your decision to follow the feeling in your gut is often the right one.

While the brain in our head is often the topic of much discourse, a little discussed reality is that our stomachs have more than 100 million nerve cells and these cells comprise a fully functioning system – the enteric nervous system.

The enteric nervous system interacts with the brain through a complex neural circuit that allows information exchange between our stomachs and brains within seconds. Although most of us view the intestinal system as primarily a digestive control function, this couldn't be farther from the truth. Most of the signals transmitted via our enteric nervous system is information *forwarded from the gut to the brain* versus information *received in the gut from the brain.* Therefore, mind gut connection is not just a metaphor – it's a reality.

In fact, given the vast amount of neural activity, scientists now say that our gut operates as a second (albeit undervalued) brain. Our second brain can influence our thinking, memory and mood as much as our heads. Consequently, the network between the brain and gut is stimulating new thinking and discourse about the role of this wildly untapped sensory pathway in areas such as weight management, mood and long-term health.

The mind-gut connection is one of the least addressed areas in business and application has yet to be applied broadly within the field of business or organizational and marketing outcomes. However, I believe the social and business conditions are necessitating new approaches, and I believe the time to understand the mind-gut connection in business is now.

Why do epiphanies matter in marketing?

At the heart of the concept of an epiphany is the inherent idea of enlightenment, realization and insight – what some refer to as light bulb moments. Ironically, marketers spend countless amounts of money and time trying to manufacture these light bulb moments, but often fall short. Why? Because, in short, these moments cannot be manufactured or replicated. Instead they are underappreciated moments of spontaneity with profound meaning.

How and why in one of the most creative professions do some leaders fail to create a brand or message that resonates while others succeed?

A fair amount centers on allowing our second brain (the gut) to begin permeating efforts versus relying solely on thoughts that emanate from the head and brain. It is as advantageous to go with your gut, as it is to go with your mind. The problem is that we, as leaders, marketers and humans forget how to listen for epiphanies and fail to trust our intuition.

I mentioned it is unfortunate that technology has become synonymous with marketing. Don't get me wrong, I fully understand the profound ways technology has influenced marketing and the diverse channels available today. I also understand the need for data and evidence – particularly in an era where digital is king.

However, I see many who have forgotten that marketing is much more than a tool, and for those who are willing to go on this journey, I'd like to show you a different way, one that embraces technology not the main event of marketing but a component of an evolving marketing mix.

Epiphanies provide new sensory pathways that lead to enlightened moments. When we are aware and receptive, these moments open us up to change and to operating in new ways. The challenge so many of us face with using epiphanies to our benefit is that these epiphanies cannot always be proven or disproven, which means we need to learn to trust *our second brains* a bit more.

At the crux of this is willingness to feel and honestly expose your organization, including those weaknesses and insecurities. And then trust that new, unconventional thinking may be the key to unlocking new success. This may just be the biggest reason to adopt an epiphany marketing mindset. Fasten your seatbelt, it will take some courage.

CHAPTER 2

Today, the intersection of organizations, fans, and technology is rapidly transforming the way the world markets and behaves.

THE ERA OF "MARKEXPERIENCE"

There have been at least four key stages of the modern marketing evolution and we are amid a fifth. As discussed by Maximilian Claessens (2018), marketing has gone through a series of evolutions and each has impacted our approach to marketing. These changes started about 150 years ago and, since that time, often coincided with significant technology introductions and generational shifts in thinking. Similarly, the next stage of marketing is being fueled by mobile technology intersecting with evolving beliefs about humanity and societal greater good. The next stage of marketing is driven and defined by the convergence of organizations, fans and technology.

I hypothesize that the changing landscape of marketing will become increasingly dependent upon our ability demonstrate our core and deliver experiences that support that core.

I coined the term "Markexperience" to refer to this new paradigm, which will require marketers to go beyond storytelling at a single point in time. Instead, "Markexperience" will require marketers to ensure their fans experience the organizational story consistently across multiple interactions and touch points. All of this is enabled (but not driven) by technology. These three pieces (organization, fans, technology) each have a specific role in the whole experience, and like a perfect triangle, one cannot work without the other.

- *Organizations.* Organizations set motion to the circuit, and they do this by establishing *belief* internally and externally around their purpose and commitment to do something that changes or influences our world. This articulation is inherently authentic. Leaders, it is important that you understand your organization and what you stand for and behind. These answers cannot be found in mirroring or mimicking what others are doing, but rather in living what you uniquely do and inspiring what others have *yet* to do.

- *Fans.* Fans provide input on the extent to which your brand message is resonating and is worthy of reciprocation (vis-à-vis their engagement with our organizations). The action of fans is solely dependent on what you and your organization do to connect with them. The purpose of your efforts centers on involving, engaging and embracing. Fans are your most important priority, and thus fans must be the starting point for all aspects of your organization's marketing (and broader decisions). The degree to which fans are agents of support and change lays solely on ways in which you bring them into your vision for change.

- *Technology.* Technology is central for two reasons. First, technology enables fans to have a means for regular engagement with your organization. Secondly, technology constantly influences the way your fans see the world and how they subsequently interact and connect with you. Since we have access to an unlimited tool set, and it is up to us to understand how to use it effectively to deliver our message – let technology be your partner.

"Markexperience" is happening now, but why?

The Role of Technology

How we market has a lot to do with how rapidly technology is evolving. Today, it is much easier and faster to find vast quantities of information via search. Think about even just a few decades back – when shopping almost exclusively entailed leaving the comfort of home to compare prices, check quality and make the purchase. Contrast that with today, where the power of technology has enabled the experience to advance. While the convenience is a consequence, the more influential impact of technology advancement has been the opening of the floodgates for choice.

Technology has made it much easier for all organizations to share what they offer, reach a broader audience, and communicate anytime. This has, in turn, muddied the proverbial waters making it increasingly complicated for fans to discern what options are best. Everything from emails, social media, and blogs, to ads and newsletters has made it faster and easier to catch the eye of millions of potential fans sitting in the comfort of their homes, looking for something new. Smart organizations realize this and are leveraging content and technology in more deliberate ways to ensure they stay top of mind and aware of changing demands.

Perhaps the biggest contribution technology brings is enabling organizations to monitor the behavior of people visiting their websites, in order to understand what they like the most, what they are attracted to, and how can they make them stay and connect. This has created an expectation for fans that organizations will understand them, know their values and behaviors, and most importantly, that organizations will interact, accordingly, based on this knowledge.

Fans increasingly expect the organizations they interact with to deliver experiences that are more personal and customized, reflective of their specific needs at any given moment.

These factors are making technology a big part of marketing today, but at the same time it is masking the real challenge. How do we go beyond reaching and genuinely connect with fans?

The Role of Fans

There are 7.5 billion people in the world, a reality that is both inspiring and daunting. Inspiring because there are numerous pathways to impact the world, but daunting because the views among these 7.5 billion are as diverse as the countries, cities, neighborhoods and families they represent.

I raise it here to say... there's no way you can attract all of them as fans. But the good news is you don't have to. You only need to reach those fans who resonate with what you say and start speaking directly to them, better than you do today.

Marketing is rapidly shifting from speaking at, to connecting (with) fans. At the heart of this change is a desire to give them a feeling of inclusivity, and inspiration to act - often in a way that motivates change. Successful marketers (and organizations) in the era of "Markexperience" will focus on delivering authentic interactions that reflect a call to action that mirrors the generational transformation happening today.

Generational marketing refers to how we best approach the practice of marketing to appeal to collective mindsets of individuals born in a specific time period. Cultural shifts occur every generation and have profound impacts on the way we think, live and act.

We are experiencing such a shift now, where shared values and broader global perspectives are becoming prominent in our societal discourse. The fact that this is also happening with such vast technology changes, is in many ways contributing to marketing landscape evolution.

Social norms and cultural shifts guide what we market and technology guides how we market.

Today, your fans have many options that reach around the globe and are exposed to individuals whose opinions can influence selection as much, if not more, than what you say directly to them. Suddenly, the world doesn't seem so big – and it isn't. Today, we think, feel and act more globally. With this expansion of thought, beliefs are more easily shared and the number groups we can share with are exponentially bigger. Ironically, the breaking down of global barriers has made humans acutely aware of the importance of their own values, standing for these values and standing out.

Consequently, fans are looking for voices and opinions that they feel reflect and mirror their own and screening out that which does not. We have moved from an era of one-to-many marketing, characterized through identification with a critical mass of homogenous audiences, to an era of one-to-one (one-to-few) marketing, which focuses on shared values and purpose (see Exhibit 1).

Exhibit 1: Generational Evolution of Marketing

Generation		Marketing Focus	Avg. # of Words to Reach
1	Baby Boomers	• Product-Centric • Broadcast • Sales	140 words
2	Gen X	• Consumer-Centric • One to many • Marketing	~75 words
3	Gen Y & Gen Z	• Humanity-Centric • 1:1 or 1:Select group • Values	~40 words

The Role of Organizations

Organizations are front and center in cultivating belief internally, as well as creating momentum externally for their mission and desired purpose. Most find, however, that articulating beliefs in a manner that resonates is more complicated than it seems. In addition to reaching more people, we are doing so in an environment that relies on fewer words, more clutter and less time to break through.

In a relatively short time period (~50 years), marketing evolved from primarily communicating via TV advertisements, where we had an average of 140 words directly telling us what to buy, to a world where we communicate via social media with less than 50 words to convey shared values and beliefs.

At this moment, you may be contemplating an important question. "How the heck do I convey beliefs and create meaningful connections with my fans, today?" And this is a good question. But a better question to ask is "how do I *first* ensure my organization is clear in who we are so we can better connect with fans?"

You see, to attract the right fans you must rethink who you are at your core and start telling inspiring and authentic stories about your beliefs. Revisit your mission, evaluate how your brand has evolved and be honest about whether you are still who you say you are.

This means courageously going with your gut, determining your truest and most authentic thoughts, and understanding how that will be brought to life in a manner that is uniquely yours – it means getting back to your core.

If you have lost sight, I encourage you to move outside of perceived boundaries whether those are how your organizations operate today, who your fans are or what your organizations need to look like. Return to the core reason you exist and bring your organizational soul to life.

Here are some practical steps to follow to transform be a Markexperience ready organization:

1. *Move from convincing fans to a focus on connection, inclusion, and fan advocacy.* Human beings tremendously desire to have and maintain personal connections with others. Successful organizations realize that marketing needs to connect with fans over the long-haul, not just a point in time.

2. *Develop fan intimacy and change the marketing mindset from episodes to relationships.* A relationship happens when fans connect with an organization and believe the organization is a good reflection of something already valued in their own lives.

3. *Focus on reciprocity.* Understand these relationships are based on shared values that are reinforced at every interaction. Meet your fans where they are and then design experiences that recognize them but also provide an opportunity to demonstrate shared beliefs, values. Keep active across all

interactions, as this shows you take the responsibility to respond to and act on feedback received from your fans.

CHAPTER 3

If I were them, what would this make me feel?

.

CREATING CONNECTIONS WITH CONTENT

Humans have an innate need to connect with others and belong. In their groundbreaking social research, psychologists Roy Baumeister and Mark Leary (1995) eloquently point out that the need to belong is the most important need that humans must fulfill, and they declared this was as much a necessity as the fundamental need for food and shelter. Human beings, they state, must maintain at least minimum amounts of positive and significant interpersonal relationships to thrive.

While this fact is not a new phenomenon, the role of connecting and belonging are critical in the evolution we see in marketing today. Your ability to connect is the single best marketing tool you will have. Fans that connect with your organization are more likely to share your story with others, support you publicly and advocate for you with others.

When connections are built upon mutual trust and reciprocity, you experience growth in those fans and, in some cases, you create a strong and loyal following.

It may be tempting to believe that incredible marketing just happens, but it starts with your focus on one important question, "how would you like your fans to experience your organization?" From there, you explore how that experience can come to life via content.

Content is often the primary conduit your fans have between you, their understanding of who you are and why they should care. This content serves as the ice breaker in the relationship you seek to build; it defines the relationships will be episodic or long-lasting.

Using Content to Breakthrough

Before you begin creating content, you must be sure of your content strategy, starting with *who's the audience for the content and why should they care*.

Imagine you need to buy a present, with a big caveat – it's a mystery gift so you don't know who will receive the present. How do you decide what to buy? If you are like most, you may opt to buy something generic that works for a broad cross-section of people. You do this out of necessity and with the awareness that a generic gift never has the same value or impact as a gift that is bought with a specific person in mind. Similarly, it is crucial that you know the fans you are trying to reach in your marketing, and only after that point can you create content that matters.

For most, the reality is that our organizations are stretched for both resources and time. As a result, we default to create generic content in effort to attract many eyes. But it is key to remember that generic content will not have the same impact. So, understanding and recognizing the type of content desired by your fans is an important element of great content strategy and development.

Let's go back to the gift analogy. Imagine you are buying a gift for your life partner. If you are like most, you will reflect on your relationship, your shared experiences and artifacts that bring that person or those experiences to life. You use the gift as a vehicle to communicate and reinforce shared experiences. Content is similar in that represents a chance to build reciprocity and to reinforce the commitment between you and fans.

A good tool to guide content development is using the P.I.E. approach – Purpose, Intention and Engagement:

1. *Create with PURPOSE.* The best content is not something that is mass manufactured or replicated, it's something you create, and it's different for every organization, since the core is unique for every single one. Your content needs to express your

core and do it in a consistent way. Focus your efforts on the value *you* are looking to communicate to your fans and how that value makes you stand out. If you start with that blueprint, then you can be sure the content you create will be authentic and addressed to the right people.

2. *Create with the INTENTION of connecting.* Use content to create a sense of belonging and shared values through stories that reflect the spirit of your organization and your fans. Determine the feeling you want fans to leave with, help them feel a part of your story and infuse your content with real and unfiltered emotion that reflects the heart of your organization.

3. *Create to ENGAGE.* Humans now have the attention span of a goldfish, which means we constantly seek the next distraction. When fans make a choice to engage with your organization, either by purchasing, donating or spending time to read your content, they are hanging out with your brand. This doesn't mean the brand has to be the coolest in the room, but darn well better be worth their time, commitment and companionship. Communication must

be engaging from the very beginning, but it should also sustain attention.

The Three I's of Content.

Creating purposeful and engaging content that connects requires you to disclose (yes, you must be open) who you are, your values and how you are a game changer. The point of your content is to generate Inertia, Influence and Insight for your organization:

- *Inertia*. This is about bringing in interested fans to trial and experience what you offer. You need people to be attracted by your content, so they will engage with it and support your purpose.

- *Influence*. Create quality content that leaves an impression on your fans. Bring in people who start to spread your message to others and will use it to build credibility within their own fan base.

- *Insight*. Listen to what your fans tell you and tailor your content to support them. To be relevant, content ought to genuinely reflect the needs of fans, as well as their desires. Most importantly, it demonstrates a shared commitment to something bigger.

Audit content existing content

Before you start creating new content, it's a great idea to examine what you might have within your asset repository and determine how (if) you can repurpose it. These assets can range from print to digital, but the goal is to take inventory and avoid reinventing content that already exists.

As you audit, ask yourself, what have you been communicating this far? How has it worked out and how you can improve its impact? BE HONEST!

Determine what matters - throw out the rest

The important thing here is to have a line of sight into what makes an impact with your fans, what keeps the relationship strong, and what best helps your organization communicate who you are, the reasons behind your existence, and what you can do to improve the world. When evaluating content, stay focused on the core message and remove content that goes against it.

Recycle, but only where it matters for fans

If something works well, if it does a good job of connecting with fans and communicates your core message, then file it away and continue to use it.

You can also use recycled content as a model to enhance messaging for vague or generic content that may not be hitting the mark.

Whatever method your organization chooses, make a commitment to never stop finding ways to optimize your message. Test, learn and repeat.

CHAPTER 4

*True marketing doesn't come from what you sell,
but from what you believe you can achieve.*

MARKETING YOUR BELIEFS

One of the founders of Revlon® Cosmetics, an icon in the makeup business, Charles Revson once said "In the factory we make cosmetics; in the drugstore we sell hope."

Revlon is a brand that was created in 1932, at a time that can undeniably be called one of the worst times ever to sell products, the Great Depression. The organization's founders, two brothers named Charles and Joseph Revson and a chemist Charles Lachman, launched with an idea to create a longer lasting, quality and lower cost nail polish that would provide variety to users. Within 6 years, the 3 men had turned Revlon into a million-dollar company, selling only their specialty nail polish (Beach, 2017).

Revlon, with their early success, began to expand and try launching new products. But after not achieving much success, they began to refocus on the organization's core products, makeup and skin care. That decision to return the company to its core brands and essence not only re-rooted the team in their core offering, but it likely is the reason behind the brand's viability for over 70 years.

The point of this story is two-fold. First, at a time in our history when it would have made sense to communicate an idea of low-cost products, the Revlon founders realized that they would only succeed when they were selling a belief bigger than the product itself or the organization. The second point, which is equally important, is that once organizations begin to stray too far from their core beliefs it is often difficult to connect with fans and the organization suffers.

When you commit to, or advocate on behalf of, a product, service or cause, what drives you?

For most people, even if they don't have the vocabulary or something tangible to support their decision, it is something instinctual or a personal connection. Or sometimes it's just that their gut that tells them this is an organization that is worth it. It may be as simple as, "you get me" or "I agree with what you are saying". Often though, what we don't see is that it is a shared belief that drives fan willingness to dive in and support.

Given the rather instinctual, subjective and not always rational nature involved in building support, sometimes organizations find that they must recommit to or reimagine their beliefs in order to connect or reconnect with their fans. This means getting in touch with what they believe and stand for, and then making a bold decision to live and breathe it.

Beliefs are emotional, real and often reflect a conviction within us, a feeling of certainty about what something means. Every person and every organization are guided by a belief system, and that belief system defines the essence of who we are (as people and organizations). Beliefs affect thoughts about our self, others, and the world at large, while also greatly influencing our emotions and our actions. Consequently, the strength of our beliefs is a pretty good indicator of success – particularly in marketing.

Why? Well it's pretty much a matter of beliefs turning into actions. Beliefs guide our thoughts. Thoughts guide how we feel and act. Actions in turn start to define our experiences, identity and essence.

Organizations are only as strong as their beliefs, and how organizations express the beliefs ultimately impacts how many, what type and with what intensity fans choose to support you. Your beliefs are what you are marketing.

Thinking about beliefs from this perspective, it is easy to understand why just creating some catchy content and hoping it will boost fans is the wrong approach.

Beliefs turned into action then become the way our benefit is expressed to, and with, fans (how does this make their life better). The beliefs instilled in our fans - both internal and external - become what they expect from us. These beliefs can either draw them to us or push them away.

The bond we create with our fans will give them the certainty that our organization, mission and purpose represent what they are seeking in the world. If we are clear in our beliefs, we will attract those who share similar beliefs.

Let's test this out a bit. When you see The Walt Disney Company™, more specifically Disney, what images come to mind and what do those images tell you about their beliefs? If you are like most, Disney elicits visuals of movies, toys, princesses, animation, theme parks, or maybe even Mickey Mouse. But you also likely imagine the happiest place on earth, magical experiences and some feeling you've had that were created by this iconic brand.

Disney is deliberate in their message and as a result, people often report feeling joy, wonderment and something magical when thinking of the brand. The success behind the organization is built into their DNA. They spend large amounts of time and investment ensuring that beliefs in creativity and innovation come to life in their movies and venues (Disney Annual Report, 2019). The Disney brand puts experiences related to their mission at the heart of all they do.

When speaking about a brand like Disney, marketers generally believe that organizations like this belong to a certain "elite" to which they don't have access. But this cannot be farther from the truth, and it is important for you to erase that limited thinking so you can start working towards building the marketing program you want to achieve. The most critical takeaway is that through clearly articulated beliefs, every organization can build a strong, compelling message or brand.

Find your organization's soul

"What is the soul of your organization?"

First, I want to be clear that this doesn't mean finding the right word. Instead, it means finding and embracing your deeper commitment, why you exist and how you express those beliefs and values.

In a term coined, "The Golden Circle", Simon Sinek asserts that while a majority of organizations know what they do (what they sell or services they offer), fewer know what sets them apart from their competition and even fewer know their greater purpose or the cause for why their organization exists. The result is that organizations, overall, are not achieving all they can and are not connecting in meaningful ways.

I think this theory should go one step beyond merely understanding why they exist and bring to life the core understanding of an organization's DNA or soul. At the heart of marketing there should be laser focus on bringing the organization values and beliefs to light.

Based on my experiences, the most successful organizations not only communicate "why" they do what they do, but they also communicate the spirit of their actions and they unapologetically bare their organizational "souls."

Organizational soul is always built from the inside of the organization and then shared out. Therefore, identifying organizational soul is an imperative for distinguishing your organizations values and behaviors (see Exhibit 2).

Exhibit 2: Organizational Soul

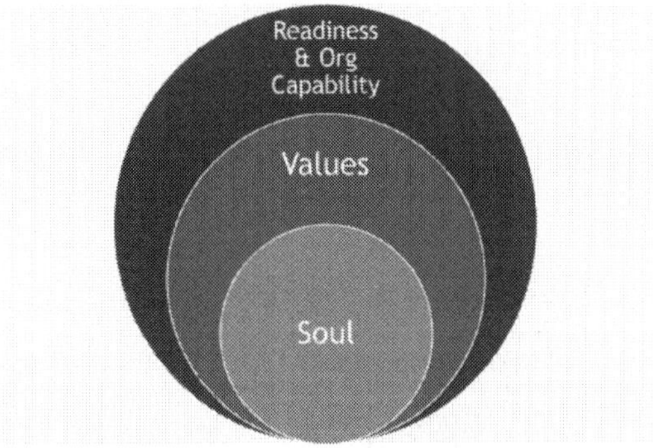

Today, we as leaders are so strapped for time and resources that we tend to lose sight of our core. We fixate on our outermost superficial layer, the layer predicated on our available resources or existing capabilities, and we then attempt to back in to our soul. This, in turn, leads to organizational reactivity. Organizational reactivity, as the name implies, means that instead of having an internal compass that guides our actions, our behaviors are dictated by the presence (or absence) of specific capabilities or resources. The availability of these capabilities and resources ultimately begins to influence various organizational behaviors, which in turn leaves organizations susceptible to the seas of change that impact all of us.

Once resources begin to drive decisions, they ultimate start to direct organizational values. These outside-in values start to permeate the internal culture, and ultimately drive our souls. Fans will notice and engagement will suffer.

Finding organizational soul requires us as leaders to begin at the center and then work our way back out to build capabilities that support the cultures we aim to create. If you find it challenging to know how to reconnect with your soul, consider the following suggestions:

- *Articulate your purpose.* If you've lost sight of your purpose, commit to rediscovery. Start with key questions like "What inspired our creation?" or "Why does our mission matter?" From here start to revisit the elements of your organization that support or detract. Then take the action required to emphasize and enhance those elements that are uniquely yours.

- *Help fans connect with your vision.* There is no straight or defined path when it comes to galvanizing fan belief in you. Because each and every organization is different, all need to define what is unique and relevant for them. Use originality and authenticity, combined with empathy to tell stories, and, where possible, to include moments with which fans can identify.

- *Live and breathe your purpose.* Remain laser focused every day on the reason why you do the work you do; this is less about what you do or how you do it and more about the beliefs you share for how the world can be different because of the vision you have. This focus must permeate your full organization so that the culture exudes it and all who touch your organization feel those values brought to life.

CHAPTER 5

We're entering a new era of marketing, where a brand's success is measured by how many people sustain a relationship

MARKETING YOUR CONTRIBUTIONS

What does it mean to market your contributions? Let's first acknowledge that we are experiencing a change in the meaning of marketing. As mentioned earlier, marketing has shifted from a focus on attracting fans that broadly resemble each other based on demographics and psychographics to meeting very specific behavioral and attitudinal needs. Moreover, the field is moving from episodic interactions to evolving and growing connections, in effort to deepen relationships.

Because of the way technology has evolved, these connections and relationships are no longer a one-way conversation, but are multi-way and multi-touch. This means your organization needs to engage in real dialogue and bring true value to the table.

Today, fans expect contribution by custodians of brands to broader discourse and/or society in a way that enhances lives. Increasingly, you will see that the focus is on enhancing the world at large, but starting with your fans is a great place to focus your energy initially.

The word contribution is inherently about giving, about sharing and about having empathy for someone (or something) other than yourself. This book was born out of the idea that I could help individuals like you understand how to improve marketing through empowering you to be bold and authentic, all while returning to your core ideology.

My contribution is boundless empowerment and the vision is that you will attain greater and meaningful success in your organizations because of it.

The best marketing happens when you stop trying to convince, and you start trying to help.

Give up the notion that you must convert and replace it with the idea of contribution. Go back to your values and organizational beliefs, share those. In these shared moments of empathy, some of your biggest epiphanies will emerge and that will be the root of your great marketing.

There are countless leaders who have found success in contribution, in fact, you will find that many leading organizations started out of a need or desire to improve life for themselves or others. Their contributions permeate our lives and homes.

One example is the founder of KIND® Bars, Daniel Lubetzy (Forbes, 2019). The son of a holocaust survivor, he made it his mission to inspire people to live kind lives. When this vision merged with his desire to find a healthier alternative to snacking while traveling – a company with a strong story to tell was conceived. Today, Mr. Lubetzy speaks about the importance of contributing positively to the lives of his fans, employees and the greater world.

One of the biggest outcomes of contribution is that it allows your organization to toot your own horn without feeling the backlash of being arrogant. Your employees, fans and the broader world want to know how you are contributing and this broadcast results in you getting more fans to not only listen to you, but to also tell your story. That's right, while some organizations are buying fans you will be able to earn hearts and minds by living your mission and contributing to society. In the case of KIND Bars, doing just this has resulted in the company reaching approximately $1 Billion revenue annually.

CHAPTER 6

Marketing today is about being steadfast in your values, then communicating and sharing those values in a way that resonates to drive commitment with your purpose.

MARKETING-WORTHY ORGANIZATIONS

Shared values are a zero-sum game, they either exist or they do not. The stakes are much higher in reaching those with whom we shared values and it will require a bigger commitment.

A great analogy for marketing today is a long-term relationship. Why? Because this is exactly what every organization should look for with fans. It's a bond that's not easily broken, built on shared values and beliefs, and mutual benefit. It endures the passing of time and ensures meaning for all parties involved.

When it comes to human connections, there's something or there's nothing. The same thing can be said of marketing, fans are either aligned with you or they are not. Given the vast amounts of options available today, alignment is dependent on the extent to which you reinforce the reasons why they should align. Specifically, fans seek to know the values you share and preferably how those values contribute to something bigger.

Let's look at Patagonia™, a designer of outdoor clothing and gear with a mission centered on preserving and protecting the environment. The company recently changed its mission to one that puts them at the helm in efforts to "save our home planet."

The company mission is more than words. The mission (Patagonia, 2019) is a living core belief and the company ensures operations back up their talk. For example, their sourcing and product materials reflect fair trade practices and are created from organic material. The company takes a very public stance in the political arena as well supporting congressional leadership who align with their company values, while criticizing publicly those whose policies are against their beliefs.

This type of authenticity speaks to Patagonia's fans who demand this type of transparency and non-neutrality on world issues that matter to them. And while this approach doesn't work for all, Patagonia has built a large fan base (and an estimated $1 Billion in annual sales) by simply living by what it says – doing whatever they can to save the planet.

The lessons from Patagonia are three-fold:

1) Identify your organization's true purpose and be consistent in telling your story. An unwavering commitment to your brand,

mission and bigger purpose will enable your organization to stand out.

2) Continuously express this shared purpose and bring that purpose to life. Don't be afraid to promote that purpose and don't be dissuaded by those fans who are not committed to your vision – the right fans will eventually come.

3) Value the various and varied interaction your story generates, and bring your fans along that journey too.

In a time where digital is pervasive in the lives of our fans, it's important to remember your fans expect you to be remarkable and consistent.

Organizations that contradict their own values or act in ways that are contrary to spoken beliefs do more harm than saying nothing. This is because fans expect that at every touch you will be the same organization and expect each experience and interaction to reinforce why they support you. The hypocrisy of those moments will easily spread, and fans won't trust that you are who you say you are.

CHAPTER 7

You will only build an audience when you create an experience that demands an audience.

~Robert Rose

EXPERIENCE IS KEY

We've covered a lot of ground thus far, so prior to summing up, I'd like to revisit some of the key ideas we've learned from the book.

- Driven by the intersection of technology along with cultural and generational shifts, we are entering the era of Markexperience. A world in which rational, thought-based approaches focused on one-to-many are being supplanted by one-to-one or one-to-few experience-based approaches that are more personal.

- Marketing success in this era is increasing defined by fan-to-organization connection, organizational fan inclusivity, engagement and action.

- Fans are demanding remarkable, consistent experiences that reinforce their alignment with organizations they choose to support.

These experiences are driven more and more by shared values.

How does an organization go about creating remarkable, authentic experiences that allow fans to be integrated and heard?

You start and finish by providing fans the stage to be award-winning supporting actors in the story of your organization. This means, you listen, value their feedback and adjust your story based on their input. In doing so, you then open the door for them to bring other fans with them.

As fans get to know you, they will develop relationships and these relationships enable you to learn more – a wonderful cycle is created.

Identify the experience(s) you want to create for your fans

More than ever fans are in search of a movement, something that makes them feel like they are involved in meaningful matters and in efforts that align to their values, thus helps them make or leave a mark. Fans, therefore, expect organizations to deliver energizing experiences that merge with their own story.

To deliver against this, you need to start at your own core and determine how you want that core to be experienced by your fans. After you've clarified your purpose, develop a brand identity (including the feeling you want to leave with your fans when they interact with you) that supports your story. From here determine your message to the world and let your fans provide input.

Find fans that align with the experience

This is about understanding your fans, developing intimacy with these fans and providing continuous opportunities to engage.

Two ways you can approach experience design are:

- *Identify an archetype.* Start by finding one example that epitomizes the ideal fan for your organization. Find an archetype who represents how you've defined your ideal fan and learn everything you can about that person. From attitudes and values to demographics and key interaction points, you use this information to attract fans who share key characteristics that are relevant for your organization.

- *Start from the bottom up.* Organizations often, erroneously, believe they must start marketing from the top down, generating awareness first and then nurturing potential fans down the funnel. Instead of thinking there is a uniform approach, I'd like you to consider a shift in focus. Experiment with different new approaches, including those leveraging a bottoms-up method – where you begin with those who care about your story, and those who are willing to share and influence others.

Encourage ongoing engagement

Get out of the way. Once you find those who care about your story and you know where to reach them. Provide a platform (and marketing channels) for them to connect with and influence others who may share the interest. Your role is then to be a catalyst for these interactions, observe, learn and adapt your marketing communication to reinforce.

This is where technology becomes critical. Use technology to understand where fans are and interact with them using the technology that aligns with how they choose to engage. Use technology as a tool to help you continue learning about what content matters, what is being said and most importantly how well your organization is authentically living your mission and purpose.

A final thought – You are unique

I want to end this book the way we started, by asking you to trust epiphanies. If you find the idea of doing this difficult, then I ask you to start by paying attention to the epiphanies that you have and begin to document them. Over time, I believe you will learn to listen for and trust those epiphanies. Ultimately, the goal is to understand and rely as much on your gut as your mind when communicating the awesomeness that you are and what you uniquely bring into the world. Trust that your distinctiveness is enough to position your organization (and you) for success.

While rationality serves us well in business, the more emotive honesty that is present with epiphanies serves as a great reminder to be who we really are and diminishes the need to be anything else. The nature of where marketing is going will require this level of honesty because fans want to follow organizations that are bold enough to say what they mean and live what they say.

EXERCISES

Exercise 1: Epiphanies in Action

I recommend you use this mental mapping exercise to get back in touch with your true organizational essence.

- Either alone or in a small group (preferably no more than 3-4 people in a group) do the following:

    - Write down the first word that comes to mind when you think of the value your organization brings.
    - From that word, create new branches of words that spontaneously come to mind.
    - From each of those words create additional sub branches
    - After you have completed 2-3 rounds of branches, review and circle the words that you believe are most representative of you today.

- Review and ask yourself if these are the words you live and breathe daily in your organization. If not, ask why and determine if you may need to reposition your organization or re-imagine your purpose.

Exercise 2: Organizational Assessment

When people interact with your organization either by purchasing, donating or engaging with your content, they are choosing to become a fan, often based on shared beliefs or values. If you don't have the right fans, want to cultivate new fans or want to engage deeper with existing fans, start by taking a fresh look at your organization by asking yourself the following questions:

- Who are you (your culture, your mission, how you behave)?
- What do you offer (what is the benefit of fans coming on this journey with you)?
- Why you do what you do (how are you changing society)?
- What impression do you want to leave with your fans?

Write down answers to these questions then ask others in the organization to do the same thing; evaluate similarities and disconnects.

To get to some of these answers I'd like you to Imagine your organization is a person.
- How does your organization behave?
- What attributes best describe you?
- Would you hang out with your brand?
- Would you trust your organization?

Exercise 3: State of Your Core

Audit 10 pieces of content (can be web, brochures, emails, etc.). Examine the state of your organization by focusing on the key message you are leaving your fans. To do so, evaluate your content through the following lens:

- *Vision and mission*: do you communicate your vision for the future and how does your mission support it?
- *Values*: do you communicate what your organization brand stands for and how those values come to life?
- *Beliefs*. How are you reinforcing your values through beliefs, related actions and other traits when interacting with fans?

When doing this exercise, focus on the following:

- Language used to discuss how you bring the mission to life, what your organization offers that is of value to fans.
- Clarity of the content.
- Consistency of the messages you share.

REFERENCES

Au-Yeung, Angel. "Social spin doctor: Kind Bar's Daniel Lubetzky builds a $1.5 Billion fortune on do-gooder rhetoric." *Forbes.* 31 Mar. 2019. 38-46. Print.

Baumeister, R.F. and Leary, M.R. (1995). The need to belong: Desire for interpersonal attachments as a fundamental human motivation. Psychological Bulletin, 117(3), 497-529.

Beach, Emily. (2017, September 26). *The history of Revlon Cosmetics.* www.bizcfluent.com

Claessens, Maximilian. (2018, March 20). *Evolution of marketing theory: From production to marketing orientation. www.*marketing-insider.eu

Cytowic, Richard. (2017, January 17). *The Pit in Your Stomach is Actually Your Second Brain: Gut feelings influence your mood and well-being.* www.psychologytoday.com

Ellett, John. (2014, September 30). *Technology is changing the future of marketing (again).* Retrieved from www.forbes.com

Forrester Consulting on behalf of StrongView. (2014). *Marketing's Big LeapForward: Overcome the urgent challenge to improve customer experience and marketing performance.* www.app.compendium.com

Patagonia Mission Statement. (2019). Retrieved from www.patagonia.com

Sinek, Simon. (2019) www.startwithwhy.com

The Walt Disney Company. (2019). The 2019 Annual Meeting of Shareholders. Retrieved from www.waltdisneycompany.com

Underwood, Emily. (2018, September 20). *Your gut is directly connected to your brain, by a newly discovered neuron circuit.* www.sciencemag.org

Zilli, Matt. (2018, February 12). *The power of shared beliefs: Market what you believe, not only what you do.* www.marketingland.com

ABOUT MAISHA

An expert in the areas of psychology and human connection, Dr. Maisha Cobb is a dynamic leader, speaker and author whose boldly refreshing ideas are redefining the field of marketing. From an early age, she had ambitions to stand up and stand out – and this key trait remains with her today.

Maisha was born in Oakland, CA and she is a three-time graduate of the University of California, Los Angeles where she completed her BA, MA and PhD. Throughout her studies, Maisha continued her work with non-profit organizations to develop programs, lead training, deliver technical assistance and champion causes at a local and national level.

Following her graduate work, she embarked on a career in marketing, where she has devoted the past 20 years building brand and marketing strategies for national and global brand leaders, spanning multiple industries. Maisha has received numerous accolades and awards for her business acumen, leadership, creative contributions and her social service involvement across the dozens of non-profit and corporate settings within which she has worked.

Challenged by a personal disillusionment with marketing and the increases in organization apathy with regard to the importance of fans, Maisha is leading the discourse on new ways to approach marketing and raising expectations for visionary organizations. Writing this book reflects a critical transition period and reconnected Maisha with her inherent interest in spirituality, interconnectedness and humanity. These principles have helped her to successfully transform organizations, particularly in her personal mission to leverage marketing as an empowerment tool for anyone or any organization committed to cultivating connections.

SPEAKING ENGAGEMENTS

If you or your organization would like a deeper dive into any of the topics discussed in this book, Maisha is available, on a limited basis, for keynote speaking and corporate presentations that will inspire change and transform the way you operate. Every effort will be made to accommodate requests, but preference will be given to organizations that are committed to being agents of change.

For more insight, please contact Maisha:

Website: https://maishacobb.com
Email: maishacobb@gmail.com
Twitter: @myito

45452915R00060

Made in the USA
San Bernardino, CA
29 July 2019